INTIMACIES, RECEIVED

ALSO BY TANEUM BAMBRICK

Vantage

Intimacies, Received

Taneum Bambrick

COPPER CANYON PRESS
PORT TOWNSEND, WASHINGTON

Cover art: Laura Burke, *Strawberry Bed,* 2017

Copper Canyon Press is in residence at Fort Worden State Park
in Port Townsend, Washington, under the auspices of Centrum.
Centrum is a gathering place for artists and creative thinkers
from around the world, students of all ages and backgrounds,
and audiences seeking extraordinary cultural enrichment.

LIBRARY OF CONGRESS CATALOGING-IN-PUBLICATION DATA

Names: Bambrick, Taneum, author.
Title: Intimacies, received / Taneum Bambrick.
Description: Port Townsend, Washington : Copper Canyon Press, [2022] |
    Summary: "A collection of poems by Taneum Bambrick"—Provided by
    publisher.
Identifiers: LCCN 2022017849 (print) | LCCN 2022017850 (ebook) | ISBN
    9781556596315 (paperback) | ISBN 9781619322622 (epub)
Subjects: LCGFT: Poetry.
Classification: LCC PS3602.A63457 I58 2022 (print) | LCC PS3602.A63457
    (ebook) | DDC 811/.6—dc23/eng/20220419
LC record available at https://lccn.loc.gov/2022017849
LC ebook record available at https://lccn.loc.gov/2022017850

98765432 FIRST PRINTING

COPPER CANYON PRESS
Post Office Box 271
Port Townsend, Washington 98368
www.coppercanyonpress.org

MIX
Paper from
responsible sources
FSC® C011935

for Chloe

CONTENTS

Intimacies, Received

1

On the trail, a newborn
grass snake bends

making half squares
as it travels past my feet.

I have learned a man I love
harmed three women before me.

No one can say more than this.
If I search for an answer

I prioritize self-protection
over solidarity. Over belief.

2

One exercise I completed in therapy:
making a list of how various partners

differed from the man who raped me.

Their names—
written down and underlined
beside each other—
like categories.

3

At eighteen, tearing off tickets
for a jazz concert, I didn't feel myself
habitually clasp and stamp
my rapist's wrist.

From photos, I knew the woman
he stood with was his fiancée.
That they were together the year before.
The day when he forced himself on me.

4

A beetle gallery is the winding
engraved track left on
the inner bark of trees
that have been bored into.

Holding out an image,
the man I love
is excited to show me.

ÉCIJA

We ate cold almond soup
between water-bearer statues.
I was gone enough
to spill raisin wine. A life
inside a life of breaking cod
to slide the bone out.
I tried sex with men
for the first time.
I had a blood stew. I cried.
You kept me with your restaurant
every night. I forgot
the book I wrote. I couldn't write.
Slivers rolled off the center
of a tethered pig's leg
with a square knife.
I was knotted after.
The doctor held my eyes.
It must be in the meat
in America. For months
antibiotics couldn't cure
the UTIs. I heard him tell you
if we had sex I could die.
You lifted water to my mouth
that night. I was willing.
You smelled my neck.
You always asked by pushing me
onto your favorite side.

LOVERS' MURAL

Days after we met, he drove us to Sevilla—
an hour through the Andalusian desert—
promised that night he would take me back.

Outside a church, a square of painted tiles stamped
to a wall of cement. *Can you find the bird in that?*
He smiled, watching me search with my hand.

Lovers stood in a flame pit. Covered their chests.
In the lower-left corner—I showed him—a swallow
coiled with gold leaves. He pointed to a plaque

I couldn't read yet: *If a woman finds this bird it means
she's with who she will marry.* He laughed, horsing
his fingers through the ties on my dress.

We bought a bottle of white wine and sat
by the street. It grew dark. He mentioned
his brother's apartment was empty.

In the car, he turned from the road home
to a lit building. The brother—his arm
around a woman's hips—tossed a set of keys.

I shook in that bathroom, translating: *Didn't we agree
you would drive me back?* I didn't know if he could listen.
If there was something off in the way that I asked.

TRAVELING

A horse tied to an old bridge. The river under it pulls
green-thin. To a woman on this train, a man whispers, *Stay with me,*

which also means, *I have no concept of what you'll leave.*
   That was what angered me.
Days ago. Gin through the carpet. Your hands drumming my knees.

How long did I think—as if biting a leash—the most important place
was the place where somebody wanted me.

Saying I Am a Survivor in Another Language

We are in the moment before we decide,
for the first time, to have sex.

We fill our mouths with salami and wine.
I am careful, peeling wax paper off glazed sponge cake

baked by nuns who live down the street.
One nun, this morning, took my hand in hers

while she told me that the most important ingredient
is the silence of prayer.

I cannot tell you this, but I held on to her
while she walked me through a village

made of thick paper. A train with a real light
and human figurines hot-glued to look

like they were heading somewhere.
I was terrified. I didn't touch a man for seven years.

Asleep. Your eyelashes open against my chest.
You are the first person to not know this.

After Picasso's *The Rape*

Rib cage, bound in shape
  as if by a stretch of skin from a pig's leg.

The first flies I see in Spain are fat-
  plucking. My street, a line of hibiscus drawn in shade.

Trash pools out from the market.
  A woman tossing a soap bucket

whispers, *There is oil on your face*
  when I walk away. I think *the mark of somebody.*

He holds tiles of bird shit
  in the tower until the bells ring, and to watch the bells ring,

he says, is like seeing a person trust
  their body over a known limit. I have felt

claustrophobic, bent in the mist
  between the river and the Alamillo Bridge.

How many times have I fought
  persistence, loosened an olive from its pit.

When we watch the sunset
  someone holds a green spotlight to one of eleven churches,

which stands out like a horn
  among hips. A gather of knuckles and thread dividing cliffs.

Willow Street

When after four years, C left,
she said I seemed unresolved about men.
That a single tragedy kept me
from fully discovering sex.
We used to pull our hair off a brush
and drop it out the window above our bed.
On a tree in the neighbor's yard, a bird
stomped that hair into its nest.
One graying square
with a mark of bright eggs in it.

Driving to Cádiz

A kind of bird like a swan but more triangular
dives and lifts behind the knives of a tractor—
five paper airplanes poking at turned dirt.

Sometimes, he wears the condom
for hours after he falls asleep. I feel carried.
His body becomes the way I think.

Not being hungry, but wanting
to halve something.

I've never finished with a man
without needing to repeat, in my head,
that I want him inside me.

We pass by piles of salt, orange cattle.
He asks me to rate the day.
We both know there's nothing emptier
than recognition in a new landscape.

DATE

Two swans paddle the length of a fountain
in a restaurant by the tourist beach.
Each with a metal band cinched to one leg
catching light as it slides between the foot and joint.
They dip their necks forward.
I imagine they are racing.
From the bar, you return with a friend
who owns a gelato chain in the city.
We kiss each other's faces.
He laughs when I say that I love ice cream.
Then, only to you in Spanish,
I could eat her face. I could eat her face.
Could she get an American girl for me?
At the end of the fountain, there isn't space
for the birds to turn their long bodies.
They hit the wall and soundlessly tear at each other's wings.
Then shake until their feathers settle. Continuing.
Underwater, polished rocks littered
with bread crusts. Coins smaller than pennies.

THE CROSS FESTIVAL

We drove to a specialist in Córdoba
after the problem spread to one kidney.
The doctor explained
infections like mine
often stem from a lack
of feminine hygiene.
In the main street, groups shared pitchers
of Sprite and Manzanilla,
paper plates sunken with paella and greens.
Did you understand? my partner asked
as we stepped out of the building.
It could be that you are unclean.
I told him, *Before you*
this never happened to me.
Ten-foot crosses of woven carnations
were suspended in patios off the street.
People danced beside them.
That day, nobody was working.
We found a table. I couldn't eat or drink.
I don't know why you are angry
he said, taking a flower off the ground
to hold out for me.

After Picasso's *Head of a Woman*

That night the neighbor's cat pawed a pigeon down
    and tore off one wing.

Whiskey glazed the glasses we kept refilling.

Across the street—more an alley, the length of my extended
    body—a woman's toes

under a stiff curtain. She mopped to a song
    about a girl tearing a flower from her hair.

I think you're supposed to think a man pinned it there.

Her daughter sat in their doorframe.
    A boy lighting her lower lip.

She smoked for the first time. I heard her ask how she looked
    holding it. With you,

I wonder what I should be. Are my hands stitched back?
    Is my face completely behind me.

The Meat Carver

Through the heavy door to the kitchen
where he works, I watch his silhouette

knifing thin slices of ham
off the glassy arc through the center of the leg

where the meat purples before the bone.
Each slice should weigh like paper if cut right.

You should see through the fat to your hand.
Each morning, he wakes before me.

He rolls the blanket inches back
to watch me sleep while he gets dressed.

ERASURE

Eating beside the wives of all his friends, I quietly order three oysters. *Disgusting,* the person beside me laughs when the half shells come over ice on a little glass plate. *That smells like a dirty woman.* Leaning together, they wonder how nauseating it must be for their husbands to go down on them. I am sitting across from a man who, in bed, turns to ask, *Are you ready?* Sometimes I am. Other times he reminds me of all the women who came so quickly with him. There is no productivity in imagining the people of my lover's past. Or to saying, here, that I am queer in a way that might puncture the conversation.

THE PUPPY AT RIVER GENIL

Nothing hurt more than that. Not the rock
forming under the skin halfway up my back.
Symptoms of geographic tongue. Not fever, weight loss—
I would sleep for days after one run.
Still, I would run covered in fleece,
through rows of chalky buildings to the river Genil.
Dammed out of shape. Farm dogs sprinted across it.
Hose water on a driveway. Farm dogs
with farmers' names branded to their hips.
Working, they sat in mud between horses.
On a walk once, you warned me
not to think of them as pets. *You look very American.*
I offered a stick to one in the grass.

Running alone, saw an orange mutt break
through a wire fence. She tore strings
from the ends of my sweatpants.
I was sure she'd been abandoned.
A rubber band around her neck. Other runners shook
their heads when I asked. I spoke terrible Spanish.
Rolling in gravel, she barked. Quick heart.
Loud breath. It grew dark. I carried her to my apartment.
We stood in the shower together. She peed
on my doormat. Coming over with a cardboard box,
you demanded that I bring her back.

Here, there aren't pounds like in Disney movies.
Why create problems when you need to rest?

At the river the next day, I looked for the wire fence.
When I dropped her, she sprinted the wrong way on the path.
I followed, but my fever was back. This is what happened
when I refused to understand. Down that road
someone would kick out three of her teeth.
I know because the police posted a photo of her curled
in an alley, looking up between bags of trash.
Watching her silhouette, I shivered by a field.
I thought I was dying. I thought: *It doesn't matter*
where I am. The drone of a raingun sprinkler
clocking over rows of short spinach plants.

FEVER

That winter—without hot water, without
a working furnace—I slept for two weeks,
waking to swallow Tylenol, to bite
at the crusts of one cheese pizza
my neighbor placed by the door for me.
Before my partner flew to Denmark with his family,
he brought the wrong medicine
saying my symptoms were like his baby's
when he had the flu. That it would pass quickly,
and I wouldn't need him. I stared off.
I lost the weight on the back
of my legs and saw triangles lift
across my tongue. This is for Maya who told
the doctor he diagnosed me wrong.
A pale green hospital room. She translated
blood test and *kidney infection* on her phone.
For Maya who canceled half a trip to cook
me carrots in butter, to sleep bent-legged
in my living room with her husband.
He doesn't care for you, she said, *come home with us.*
For my partner, the best part of sex was resting
after: his hand on my head on his chest.
Heat traveling my lower abdomen.
I became immediately sick—my body,
like a friend, reacting against him.

PARTNERS

When I had sex with him, I got sick.
For the majority of a year I suffered at least
one kind of infection. I was instructed to sleep
with a capsule of boric acid inside myself.
A doctor said, *This could kill someone*
if they swallowed it, but I already knew.
In Tucson, I mixed it—a rubbery powder—
with sugar and water in bottle caps.
Scattered those near cracks where cockroaches
rose from the basement. At night,
they preened their wings with poisoned legs
before returning to their nests. *You can understand*
why you cannot receive oral sex.
Some bodies are not compatible.
It can take years for the woman's to adapt.

DATING

My partner's mother takes me to buy a special chicken
from a man in the country.
He steps out of his house and hands her a plastic bag.
The wet body of a plucked bird
already tearing holes in the seam.
I understand her when she tells him I am American.
That his farm is certainly unlike home
for me: its triangle in the grass
where two turkeys screech,
biting the base of a barbed-wire fence.
The spot under the clothesline
that held the chicken as its blood
let over a slab of concrete.
I would like to be what she knows of women.
Smiling, they expect me to scream.

New Year's Eve

At midnight, we chew twelve green grapes
in the seconds between church bells ringing.
I am with my partner's extended family
swallowing competitively around a glass table
until our little white bowls empty.
No one can speak. We are all concentrating.
His mother pulls my hand under hers
to sneak a red lace thong, which I drop
and watch unfurl on the ground
like a napkin burning. Everyone laughs but me.
The brother, the grandfather. We are all
still choking. *This is tradition,* it takes a while
for her to tell me, *wearing red for your partner*
—her son—*on New Year's Eve.*
This is how you spend the rest of the year lucky.

INSPIRATION

We waited at the Hemingway bar in Ronda
   with the little "bandit" museum outside.

You joked I was a bad American
   for not wanting to go to the bullfight.

*There's the kind with the stabbing at the end and the other
   where the bull doesn't die.*

You thought the second might get me to write.
   I asked, *Would there still be bullfights without tourists?*

Holding a glass of whiskey, I remembered the *New York Times*
   neutrally describing cultural value

and profit pitted against animal rights.
   You bundled salami off a plate and sighed.

I am sorry I tried to help with your poems. Then, smiling,
   I'd like to be worth your time.

COUNTRYSIDE

One sister holds a lighter under the paddle of a prickly pear.
    The other chants *Fire, fire!*

Their grandfather pokes pig cheeks vibrating over charcoal,
    a hand-sized radio to his ear. He frowns about Catalonia.

He says to me, *You can't understand what this means here.*
    The breaking of a reset bone. His wife, Maria,

throws two jump ropes over an olive tree
    and ties a swing. When she laughs I imagine

washing clay from a glass, or forty years
    of happy smoking. I am vaguely aware of a history:

that it's offensive—but not why—to play the version of the Spanish
    national anthem that includes singing.

We sit on a blanket. Eat bloody meat. Everywhere I go
    young people think the old are guilty.

Maria blows into a blade of grass to get the dog going.
    Do you know what I mean when I say we are still open

from the past, she asks—pulling at an orange and passing—
    or how a flag can carry with it a kind of stink?

LEGEND

The city Écija was once a beautiful woman.
Her body permanent between
a mule ranch and hills of old olive trees.
The story starts with her falling
in love with the sun. The story
starts with the sun's fixation
on her virginity. With all the rivers
drying up. Insects crawling
for scraps with burned-off wings.
They say the city and the sun
could not come close enough.
That touch was so insufficient
it became infuriating. They wanted
into each other. The destruction
of a complete understanding.

In desperation, they met with the devil,
who granted the city twelve towers
tall enough to pierce and hold the sun.
It would feel, the devil promised,
like their bodies had been stitched together.
If the union was severed
he would claim them.

For a moment, they were bound.
A thrashing energy, enormous,
collapsed in its own net.
But this was not the will of God.
As punishment he soon struck
one tower in half, which only the city felt

the way stags must
when antlers snap off their heads.

No one attempted to rebuild the tower
for hundreds of years.
Charred stone. Wood planks
exposed and sloughing off ash.
And tourists who trace the damage.
Who imagine God
when they smell their hands.

5

At the top of the bluff
our knee blood collected
on the heads of chamomile plants.

I know it's wrong
every time I feel further from
an idea of queerness.

6

In a Picasso Museum,
I saw rape depicted
as a series of charcoal drawings.
I bent my legs.

I learned this in choir practice:
if an audience causes you panic,
how not to faint.

7

Who was it who laughed when he said

All independent lesbian films end
with the lead going back to men.

More than love, I choose disappointment.

On the Nightstand, a Bowl of Fabric Roses

Behind our apartment an old river
and, behind that, a field of hived bees.

From bed, a horse we could watch—freckled gray—
walking the circle permitted by a long leash.

Each morning a farmer came, hammering
the metal stake she was roped to a few feet over.

We were having sex when you asked if we could get married.
Because I waited to say yes, you stopped moving.

AFTER TOYEN'S *SAD DAY*

When the wind picked up, the field dried.
The window. The sound
of apples blowing from a tree.

Sex was the first thing
someone else took away from me.

Cold Week

when I learned to speak   neighbor blowing smoke

    crumbled balcony   little dog head

horn music   a dark empty   stars

    puncturing   the weight of a man's body

five-foot candle   by the restaurant

    he finished outside me   prayer song

    coins   gathered at my knees

incense rocked through   handmade human figurines

ALLIGATORS: AN ESSAY

Is it scary living in Spain because of the men? a friend asks. I think for a minute. I do remember the library inside a mansion with a glass ceiling. A middle-aged man sitting across from me, staring. The library sat in the corner of the plaza where I once saw a cat eat a bundle of pink chicks after the wind knocked their nest from a tree. I was twiddling a red pen, and he copied me, trying to get my attention. He whispered, *Are you an English teacher,* and I nodded, gripping my computer. *Where?* he asked, and I pointed down the street to the high school, sunk in mud by the flooded river. *Titanic,* he understood, and I smiled because that's what the students called it. *I have to teach a private lesson,* I said, and he watched me exit the building.

———

That spring, I left Spain for five days to go to a writers conference in Tampa, Florida. I waited under a palm tree beside a freeway that skirted the beach. An Uber driver pulled up, already smiling. *Hello,* I said. *Thank you for coming so far to get me.* He gave me a bottle of water and watched me drink. Said he'd been a teacher all his life until a recent change. He asked if I was a writer like all the others he'd met that week. *Yes,* I said. He asked about my poems, which I described as focused on gender and sexuality. *Sexuality,* I remembered too late, is a word you can't use outside of academic settings. He told me I was the most interesting person he'd ever met. He reached my destination and kept driving. *What if I take you to Orlando? What if we go to the other side of the state? I won't charge you, keep talking to me.*

———

As I exited the library, I heard the man calling *Maestra! Maestra!* down the street. His voice filling the space between close buildings. I held my head through my hair. I said what I hoped meant *Leave.* I tried: *I don't speak Spanish, I don't have time.* He laughed, running. I ran, too. Papers with types of birds on them melting into my chest. I reached the family's home and pressed the button. Pressed the button. Pressed the button. When I shut the door, I threw it like an exhausted weapon.

———

Every Wednesday, I gave English lessons to a little boy and girl in their home. I played games with them, making words into actions. Taped photographs of animals onto a globe in the countries of their habitats. I said the name of the animal in English, and they impersonated it. Two butterflies floating through the kitchen. Monkeys scratching each other's back. Sometimes, when they seemed calm enough, I'd let them be big. Alligators were their favorite. Together, we learned that the word likely evolved from early Spanish colonization in Florida. That many believe it is an evolved mispronunciation of *el lagarto,* which is Spanish for "the lizard." *ALLIGATORS!* I'd scream, and their arms became mouths crushing the arm of a couch. They roared like angry lions. We did this until their mother came in and eyed the tutor snarling with her children on the ground. Then we had to be small: dogs and cats, pigeons. Anything the children could see where they lived.

———

Before I arrived in Spain, people warned that it would be very dangerous. They had words for Spanish men: *beautiful, aggressive, seductive, alluring.* My sister and her partner bet I'd get married. Even the representative from the Spanish Consulate in Seattle, when he met me at a Starbucks to discuss my visa, said, *I guess I won't be seeing you again.* He had watched many American women fall in love with Spanish men. I had just left a three-year relationship with a woman and felt annoyed by his presumption. In conversations like this, I saw people doubt my self-awareness and intellectual ability. I smiled and laughed. Tried to explain that I was interested in learning Spanish, in part to meet the second-language requirement for PhD programs. I reminded many people that I grew up in a country governed by terrifying men. Men are terrifying.

———

When I started dating a man in Andalucía, I knowingly fell into the narrative placed on me before I left. On March 8, 2018, while I was in Tampa, 5.3 million Spanish women organized a national walkout, demanding equal pay and other basic forms of gender equality. My partner, a Spanish man, called and mentioned it to me. *I don't understand what they have to complain about,* he said. *Most women don't even work. I would kill to live like that.* I pressed my face against the hotel window. I was jet-lagged; it was 5:00 a.m. The sunrise snapped back at me from the purple glass of a hotel across the street. I could really hear, then. I spoke Spanish. I had just told him about the Uber driver, which I connected, for him, to how I felt when the man chased me from the library.

————

In Florida, Georgia, Texas, and Louisiana, people pay to watch professionals wrestle alligators at amusement parks. I have participated in this. When the alligators are reluctant to fight, they are sometimes hit on the head with sticks. People take airboat rides in swamps and toss marshmallows into the water, hoping to see the stony nubs of alligator eyes surface. Alligators raised in rusted tubs like hatchery fish. Alligators that have their jaws forced open so that entertainers can toss sand on their tongues, triggering their impulse to snap shut. That's what people pay to see. Teeth. An incomprehensible potential for violence.

————

I learned the Spanish word for "monster" early because I used it to teach my two students their colors, shapes, and parts of the face. They listened to my instructions and drew accordingly. Three square heads. Covered in scales. Orange, green, pink. Every lesson they asked for this. Their parents taped the monsters across the center of their fridge. One night, an older man eyed my partner while we ate in a bar. He raised his beer and yelled the word *monstruo!* My partner acknowledged him by laughing, tilting his own glass. Because of the way men often talk about women—like changing objects—I immediately wondered if this term was in reference to what might happen between the two of us. What was he like before we met? I spent the rest of the night imagining situations that would warrant such a description. I felt myself sinking into the realization that I didn't know the person I was with. He became instead the man who assaulted me. For a while I was quiet and then I told him I didn't feel well. For days we barely spoke until he pieced together what could have happened and told me that, in Spain, the word *monster* can also mean *friend*.

———

It took seven years for me to sleep with a man after I was assaulted. I find it difficult to watch TV and popular movies where sex is presented alongside violence. I am rarely comfortable having conversations with straight men.

———

When I met my partner, he mentioned that he owned a restaurant. In a tiled room hung with dim lights, he made me paella and spinach mousse. Drizzled raspberry compote over sponge cake baked by local nuns. For the first two months, we only shared dinner. Smiling at each other between old statues. Google translating us in its robot woman voice. We spent hours making faces at each other across different tables. It seemed like this could be a life.

One morning, several months into our relationship, I woke to a message calling me back home for a writing fellowship. He turned to his phone to research it himself. Recognizing the university, the funding, and some of the authors it produced, he agreed I had to go. Holding my hand under the tight sheet, he asked if I was willing to try long-distance. *It's two years,* I said. He smiled and kissed my head. It crushed me.

———

There was a night during the writers conference in Tampa—a bamboo-covered wall, 3:00 a.m.—I met a man sitting alone at a bar by a giant, fanned leaf. I was angry about the earlier conversation with my partner in which he denied the prevalence of sexism in Spain. Back home, the man in Tampa lived with a serious partner. It was unusually cold by the beach. He read and understood my poetry. I let him walk me to where I was staying.

———

The next morning on a ten-hour layover, the memory uncurled in my head. Distracted, I lost my wallet somewhere between the bathroom and a restaurant where I ordered too many drinks. My backpack slumped beside me like another body. The waitress was tired of feeling angry. She clenched her teeth: *I have to decide if I need to call the police.* I started crying, running around the airport looking while she held my phone as a guarantee. An hour later, a middle-aged man crouched beside me (I was on my hands and knees scanning under a row of seats). My wallet in his hand, he mispronounced my name. I hugged him, feeling lifted from a collision of feelings. I wanted there to be someone to talk to about the rules I'd broken the night before, about how the man in Tampa told me he would marry me if things were different. The moon on the windows of an empty street. In thirty hours, I would walk out of the Málaga airport, stunned by the light. When my partner picked me up there, he paid to park his car so he could see me sooner, so he could kiss me without blocking the cars in line.

———

In a restaurant after, eating sardines off skewers, I tried not to think about the man in Tampa. When I thought about him my eyes swelled. I felt desperate. Throughout those last months in Spain, I became the kind of person who could bend around a lie. Selfish, predatory, looking for ways to preserve myself. Trying to convince myself that it didn't mean anything because it happened so far away. Because they were both men, and were probably using me, too, in their own ways and for different reasons. Because no one is capable of monogamous love. And under that action, I was really just demonstrating that I didn't want to move back to Spain after the fellowship. To be my partner's wife and an English tutor for the rest of my life. I was trying to force myself to write.

After I left Spain, my partner bought a ticket to Miami—for four months away—as a surprise. He invited his best friends. I felt if I changed my mind about the trip, about my guilt, about long-distance with him, I would leave twelve people who didn't speak English to fend for themselves on a tour around the country I lived in. What I remember about Florida is that none of his friends believed in the US moon landing. They walked around the NASA John F. Kennedy Space Center raising their eyebrows at one another. They winked. When I took them to the Everglades, they reacted similarly to a pile of alligators sleeping behind a chain-link fence: *Robots! Can you believe Americans are so trusting?* A muscular woman slid between us and opened a bucket filled with white, dead rats. I could hear her cracking their spines in her hands. She tossed them into the pit. The alligators came alive then. His friends screamed, gripping the fence. Slabs of concrete toppled into the pond, scratching one another's armored skin.

Because of the way bodies negotiate around trauma, most of what I remember about the man who assaulted me are the things he did beforehand. I registered them as romantic. He was in college and I was in high school. Because he loved me, he said, it was impor-tant to him that he protect my reputation from scandal—a girl in a small, conservative town. Our relationship had to be secret. He attended a university two hours away. I learned various halfway points on forest roads where we could meet in one of our cars, usually at night. He wouldn't go with me to prom but asked that I meet him after, on the mountain pass, still in my dress. I took my shoes off to walk to his car across a parking lot at 3:00 a.m. Snow still on the ground. I believed these weekend meetings were a sacrifice for him, especially because I stated that I was not ready to have sex.

I later endured a long process of learning that these actions I associated with love were often small forms of attack. Wanting to forgive him, I carried a terrible heat in my chest.

———

Over Christmas break one year, he entered my parents' house while we visited my grandparents. The house sat at the end of a long gravel driveway, a square between cow fields. The door was always unlocked, even when we left for extended trips, a thoughtless revelation, which to him registered as permission to walk into my bedroom and look through my dirty clothes. He left the cloth bracelet he always wore on my pillow without a note; it smelled intensely like him. He later said he liked the underwear that had cherries on it the most. Instead of feeling angry, I was both flattered and afraid. I explained in desperation that my friends and I—while thirteen years old—had bought matching thongs together as a joke. I was ashamed about how young I must have seemed to him as he dug through my childhood bedroom alone.

———

The Everglades are pocketed with deep depressions that alligators make and hide in during colder months. Gator holes. Limestone ponds filled with water and vegetation. Alligators lie suspended in mud, eyes open or asleep. Bodies entrusted to the structures they build.

———

Before leaving Miami, I said goodbye to my partner in a hotel room. I knew it was the last time I would ever see him. I wondered if he knew it, too. He didn't want to have sex. Not with his friends waiting in a van. An air conditioner blowing useless strings toward our calves. *Please,* I asked again. I didn't understand what I needed from him. He kissed me. I held the weight of that year, a mess of shame and appreciation. He let me live in his apartment. I wasn't in love, but I was almost sure that, had I thought about it differently, I could have been. Steeling myself against what was easy to identify as danger. What I learned about men. Something in them that made them capable of deception and rape. I wasn't sure if feeling that way had protected me or justified my erratic behavior, allowing me to become less of a person.

———

Every Wednesday my senior year in high school, I sat in a therapist's office in a little tower above the town square where I grew up. With a Walkman in my hands, I listened to birdsong on a low volume. The therapist—a blond woman who wore a memorable amount of silver bracelets and rings—would loudly read off a list of events. After reading each one, she looked to see if I nodded my head. When I nodded, I signaled that I accepted the event: it happened to me, my body lived through it. The list was chronological, starting back in my childhood. *When you were five you stood on a frozen pond in an arboretum with your mother, she held your hand.* I would nod *yes.* Most of the memories were innocuous. Toward the end she would read off the descriptions of the day when I was raped, which included sensory details—the way the car smelled, the heat, what I could see through the window—triggering a dramatic but supervised panic attack.

Aside from the event that brought me there, these are the worst hours I have lived. But, because of them, I rarely had panic attacks outside of therapy sessions. I developed coping mechanisms to practice on my own. One of those mechanisms was refusing to sleep with men for seven years. Another that seemed frustratingly simple when my therapist presented it was to make a list of how each man I knew was different from the one who assaulted me. The cars they drove, the food they liked, the color of their hair, how they spoke to and about women. Still, as an unhealthy but ingrained method of self-protection, I look for ways in which all men resemble him.

———

Alligators can lose and grow up to 3,000 teeth in their lifetime.

———

I was raped when I was seventeen. There were times when, feeling incapable of love and social interaction, I was too exhausted to imagine a future with anyone. Nobody helped me through my fear or taught me to stop acting in ways that were occasionally irrational, even violent. I survived. Because nothing worse could happen than my not wanting my life.

Intimacies, Received

Having you was like having a baby.
    A box of matches carrying bees across a lake.

I keep the reel of your passport photo
    in my coat pocket, bent around a coin.

There were many nights when you threatened to run away.
    If falling in love is a decision,

I listened for the click in your breath.
    You aren't old enough to know yet

few people have your best interest
    at heart. At heart, I swept the wet glass

of you throwing pills across the street.
    When you were sick, I wrote your weight

in kilograms so you wouldn't understand
    what was happening.

Were you with women because you were afraid of men? The men you knew were young. All young men start before they ask. Send boxed flowers. Plastic studded in sweat. Every woman I've been with was once with a young man. I understand rape. I would like to introduce you to my family. Take you to where Iberian bulls lie still on the beach. We could walk right up to them. Huge nostrils pushing out columns of steam. There will be a day when I can no longer. Both of our eyes are green. Between two women, isn't an intensity lacking? I broke down the spiderweb banging against your window. Its trap of rain and old leaves. With me, you can have whatever history. Don't tell my mother. Let me carry the heaviest grocery bag. Since I've known you you've seemed afraid of your life. I am an example you won't let yourself have.

Imagine how much you will love me
when I become easier to understand.
You don't know it, but when you speak
in Spanish you sound like a famous gay man.
A little bad, in the church, not using
the right words for heat. I know you are American
because of the way you push your fork
against meat. Because you were slow
to sleep in my bed, I loved you different.
How do you translate that? Standing in the street
ringing your doorbell made me mad.
On what I thought was our first date
you thought you'd been kidnapped—
that would be a good story to tell at a wedding.
Everybody wishes they had what we have.
Aren't you learning another language, having dinner
for free? If you stay you could live
one month a year with your family.
When they visit we'll roast sardines
on the world's cleanest beach.
You could manage my restaurant,
our wine festival. The weekly dance.
I know you, I understand. I could be anyone
and you'd still want your life back.

———

When you write about me you will call me the old bald ugly monster. I am sure. The worst man in Spain. You will say we never went anywhere together. That I fed you little hamburgers. Locked you on the balcony in the rain. We had the worst sex. My cock smaller than your American erotic thing. You only write when you have a sad story. I will have to keep you very happy. With me you are a mother already. My son learning English for free. Here, everyone loves you because it is very cute when you speak. If we get married. In Portugal, the storks are so loud it sounds like clapping. I could wait two years if you need. The cowboys in your country. If you don't love me, please. There has never been anything like this. You could still write on the side. I make enough money to take all the responsibility from your life.

Oven Street

Beside my apartment there was a church
with three lines of gold in its ceiling.

A little white dog that bit
a door handle, letting herself out to pee.

Two women who, every night, cried laughing
while they smoked. Their smoke

coming in through the window made it difficult
to be on top of you, breathing.

When we met, I knew
exactly how long I would be happy.

8

Out a tall window
one drift boat turns toward the bank.

I love you
if I don't think about
who you were before me.

9

When I worry you are angry
I am angry.

You aren't thinking about me.

Someone's favorite music
in the car. We watch Sevilla
through a bent railing.

10

In a parking lot

head-sized rocks thrown
to the weeds.

The paddle of a prickly pear
snapped down the center.

White like Styrofoam
leaking whiskey.

11

I receive a message where B claims

you aren't a real artist
because you don't write every day.

He was the first man I tried to sleep with.
When I pushed him off, he came beside me.

The stem of an indoor plant
thicker where it bent
across the ceiling.

12

Because I asked, C once admitted
that I was not the most attractive person
she had been with.

She had better sex with someone else.

I cried in the bathroom at the coffee shop where I worked
until I realized honesty was something I'd never felt.

13

You push your palm against my face in bed.
I imagine this is you asking for space.

I am trying to warm up your nose, you say.

We laugh so hard,
but I have shown you something.

Acknowledgments

BOAAT: "Erasure" (as "Bisexual Erasure"), "On the Nightstand, a Bowl of Fabric Roses"

Fairy Tale Review: "Legend"

Four Way Review: "Partners"

Mississippi Review: "Dating," "Driving to Cádiz," "Fever"

Missouri Review Online: "Traveling"

Moss: "Untitled: 13" (as "Diary Entries")

The Nation: "Saying I Am a Survivor in Another Language"

The New Yorker: "Intimacies, Received"

Poetry Daily: "Saying I Am a Survivor in Another Language"

Poetry Northwest: "Date," "Lovers' Mural"

32 Poems: "After Picasso's *Head of a Woman*"

Verse Daily: "After Picasso's *The Rape*"

Washington Square Review: "Oven Street," "Willow Street"

West Branch: "After Picasso's *The Rape*," "The Cross Festival," "Écija" (as "Écija, Notes")

Thank you to my friends for their feedback and/or encouragement: Aria Aber, Ashley Dailey, Belinda Huijuan Tang, Benjamin Schaefer, Bryan Byrdlong, Caitlyn Alario, Cherline Bazile, Claire Meuschke, Colby Cotton, Dorothy Chan, Dujie Tahat, Emily Lee Luan, Gabrielle Bates, Iqra Cheema, Jay Deshpande, Jenny Molberg, Jess Abughattas,

Jessica Lee, Joy Priest, Jos Charles, K. Iver, Luther Hughes, Katharine Whitcomb, Maya Zeller, Natasha Rao, Patrycja Humienik, Sofia Fey, Tomás Morín, Vince Granata, and many others.

Thank you to the editors who supported this project at early stages, especially Keetje Kuipers and Kevin Young. To the 2020 cohort at Stanford University for our community: Colby Cotton, Jay Deshpande, Monica Sok, and sam sax. To the cohorts before and after ours for the same thing: Claire Meuschke, Courtney Kampa, Derrick Austin, Esther Lin, Graham Barnhart, Hieu Minh Nguyen, Jim Whiteside, J.P. Grasser, Richie Hoffman, and Safia Elhillo.

To A.I. Ross. To my family: Cathy, Dale, and Chloe Bambrick.

Thank you to Elaina Ellis, John Pierce, Claretta Holsey, Michael Wiegers, Marisa Vito, Ryo Yamaguchi, the Publishing Interns, and everyone at Copper Canyon Press.

Lastly, thank you to my professors at the Stegner Fellowship: Eavan Boland, Louise Glück, and Patrick Phillips. To my professors in the University of Arizona MFA program: Susan Briante, Farid Matuk, and Ander Monson. To Bread Loaf Writers' Conference—especially De'Shawn Charles Winslow—and the Vermont Studio Center for their support. To my cohort and friends at the University of Southern California, for what we're writing now.

ABOUT THE AUTHOR

Taneum Bambrick is the author of *Vantage,* which received the 2019 American Poetry Review/Honickman First Book Award. A 2020 Stegner Fellow at Stanford University, she has received support from the Bread Loaf Writers' Conference, the Environmental Bread Loaf Writers' Conference, the Sewanee Writers' Conference, and the Vermont Studio Center. Her work has appeared in *The New Yorker, The Nation, PEN,* and elsewhere. She is a Dornsife Fellow in Creative Writing and Literature at the University of Southern California.

Poetry is vital to language and living. Since 1972, Copper Canyon Press has published extraordinary poetry from around the world to engage the imaginations and intellects of readers, writers, booksellers, librarians, teachers, students, and donors.

COPPER CANYON PRESS WISHES TO EXTEND A SPECIAL THANKS TO THE FOLLOW-
ING SUPPORTERS WHO PROVIDED FUNDING DURING THE COVID-19 PANDEMIC:
4Culture
Academy of American Poets (Literary Relief Fund)
City of Seattle Office of Arts & Culture
Community of Literary Magazines and Presses (Literary Relief Fund)
Economic Development Council of Jefferson County
National Book Foundation (Literary Relief Fund)
Poetry Foundation
U.S. Department of the Treasury Payroll Protection Program

WE ARE GRATEFUL FOR THE MAJOR SUPPORT PROVIDED BY:

academy of
american poets

THE PAUL G. ALLEN
FAMILY FOUNDATION

amazon literary
partnership

CULTURE

the point
envision·enact·evolve

Lannan

A&

ART WORKS.

National
Endowment
for the Arts
arts.gov

OFFICE OF ARTS & CULTURE
SEATTLE

WASHINGTON STATE
ARTS COMMISSION

The Witter Bynner Foundation
for Poetry

TO LEARN MORE ABOUT UNDERWRITING
COPPER CANYON PRESS TITLES,
PLEASE CALL 360-385-4925 EXT. 103

WE ARE GRATEFUL FOR THE MAJOR SUPPORT PROVIDED BY:

Richard Andrews

Anonymous (3)

Jill Baker and Jeffrey Bishop

Anne and Geoffrey Barker

In honor of Ida Bauer, Betsy
  Gifford, and Beverly Sachar

Donna Bellew

Matthew Bellew

Sarah Bird

Will Blythe

John Branch

Diana Broze

John R. Cahill

Sarah Cavanaugh

Stephanie Ellis-Smith and
  Douglas Smith

Austin Evans

Saramel Evans

Mimi Gardner Gates

Gull Industries Inc. on behalf of
  William True

The Trust of Warren A. Gummow

William R. Hearst III

Carolyn and Robert Hedin

David and Jane Hibbard

Bruce Kahn

Phil Kovacevich and Eric Wechsler

Lakeside Industries Inc. on behalf
  of Jeanne Marie Lee

Maureen Lee and Mark Busto

Peter Lewis and Johnna Turiano

Ellie Mathews and Carl Youngmann
  as The North Press

Larry Mawby and Lois Bahle

Hank and Liesel Meijer

Jack Nicholson

Gregg Orr

Petunia Charitable Fund and
  adviser Elizabeth Hebert

Suzanne Rapp and Mark Hamilton

Adam and Lynn Rauch

Emily and Dan Raymond

Joseph C. Roberts

Jill and Bill Ruckelshaus

Cynthia Sears

Kim and Jeff Seely

Joan F. Woods

Barbara and Charles Wright

In honor of C.D. Wright,
  from Forrest Gander

Caleb Young as C. Young Creative

The dedicated interns and
  faithful volunteers of
  Copper Canyon Press

The Chinese character for poetry is made up
of two parts: "word" and "temple."
It also serves as pressmark for
Copper Canyon Press.

This book is set in Athelas.
Book design by Gopa & Ted2, Inc.
Printed on archival-quality paper.